Return of the OBSERVER

by

MÁRQUEZ PRICE

D E D I C A T I O N

Gratitude to everything observed.

TABLE OF CONTENTS

P R E F A C E

In the expansive mosaic of human experience, there are threads that weave through the fabric of our lives, forming our perceptions and illuminating our paths. From the dust-filled streets of ancient Egypt to the dizzying heights of our fears, from the tender embrace of parental love to the stark simplicity of digital detox, each thread offers its own tutorials, its own revelations.

In this collection of essays, I embark on a journey of exploration and introspection, guided by the tapestry of observations drawn from diverse corners of existence. From the sun-soaked landscapes of Egypt to the inner landscapes of the human soul, I journey across realms both external and internal, searching to unknot the questions that lie hidden within.

Through the lens of travel, I witness the majesty of ancient civilizations and the enduring power of human creativity. Through the lens of fear, I confront my own vulnerabilities and discover the strength that lies dormant within me. Through the lens of parenthood, I experience the profound depths of love and sacrifice that shape our identities.

As you journey through the pages of this book, you'll encounter moments of digital detox and minimalism, where the cacophony of modern life fades into the background, allowing us to rediscover the simplicity and serenity that reside at the core of our being. I explore the transformative power of gratitude and empathy, discovering how these simple yet profound practices can enrich our relationships and deepen our connections with others.

In each essay, I invite you to pause, to reflect, and to embrace the wisdom that emerges from the act of observation. For it is through observation that we come to understand ourselves and our place in the world, and it is through understanding that we find meaning and purpose in our lives.

May these essays serve as beacons of insight and inspiration, guiding readers on their own journeys of self-discovery and transformation.

SILENT SPECTATOR: CHRONICLES OF OBSERVATION

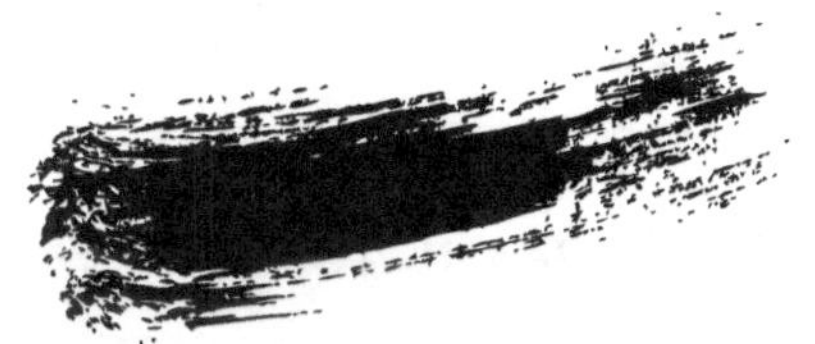

Life in the Pandemic: A personal story of adaptation.

Amid what seemed like an onslaught of sheer chaos in a myriad of ways, at the behest and caprice of March 2020 worldwide, I found preference and solace from a statement of a close friend. Being that this friend is as high strung of a person as anyone will ever encounter. I gravitated to him at the beginning of the Covid19 pandemic because I knew he'd serve as a linchpin of survival. As the research extraordinaire who will question, refute, and validate concerns that necessitate attention. On this day he told me, "This thing isn't going anywhere for a long time" when talking about the Corona virus. Which was also a softer way of saying that our collective notion of normalcy was disappearing fast with no near sight of return. Alas, America was now leveraged by a plight it usually dismisses on the news as unfortunate, yet out of the reach of its first world comfort. This dilemma blanketed the planet, as prevalent as the stars put our nights to bed with a moon's vantage point that we could finally see that we are all tied together, albeit by the strings of an indiscriminate threat.

My usual and reliable ironclad optimism had started to wane after the first couple months of the world being shaken up like an ant farm, but my response to my friend was rooted in what I store as a back up to that optimism- a resolve that prepares me to never back down from a challenge. I joke about this imaginary battery with friends of other races as one black people have learned to store in our backs through our experience in America. So, I responded with, "I don't care if this goes on for the next twenty years, I'm going to come out of it unrecognizable." At the time, I had started to let my hair grow out again and I was working out with religious fervor doing calisthenics and hiking since all the gyms were shut down. The drive fueling that statement had nothing to do with any assumption of it pertaining to an outcome attached to physical appearance. I was shadowed by the same fears, insecurities, and uncertainty as everyone else that assailed me in the forms of insomnia, worry and periods of helplessness. The difference was that I saw the time as an opportunity to reset many aspects of my life and ensure that they were changed for the better with a tag of longevity. Following are some of the things I made a choice to revamp to give myself a sporting chance in the face of any obstacle.

The first thing for me was armoring a healthy lifestyle with more discipline. I've always been consistent, not perfect, with maintaining a healthy lifestyle, but I placed greater emphasis on my eating habits, workout regimen and thoughts through mindfulness. I'd be lying if I said at that time, that I always ate healthy, pushed myself past the inevitable workout plateau or thought from a place of clarity on a daily then. I mimicked the occasional frequency of the fear, insecurity, and uncertainty I mentioned earlier that was plaguing the globe. I vacillated between extremes of an Instagram fitness guru and Jeff Lebowski.

I indulged the chicken wing, carne Asada and mini chocolate donut binges following strenuous hikes as balance because I rationalized that it assuaged and rewarded the noise outside of my quarantined bubble, but my thoughts always brought me back to a needed shift in trajectory overall. The inception of that shift came from a conversation with a friend of mine serving football numbers in the penitentiary on a phone call. He asked me how it was on the outs with this pandemic in which I said, "Man, dawg...it's like prison. Everything is shut down. Social distancing, no gathering and..." He cut me off, "say, walk to your door and open it. You can walk in and out. Don't ever confuse that with serving time, homie. Serve your time during this pandemic with discipline and that time will serve you." My mindset changed from there.

Being that I was living in a house by myself with a dog as my companion, I decided to convert potential quarantine loneliness into an inordinate amount of time afforded to focus on all facets of my life with a fortunate option of working remote when I wanted through my career. I grabbed a notebook and decided to write everything down that I ate daily, along with my physical activity, meditation and reading to serve as a log. I devised a "five-two" method that would ensure that I ate by the book Monday through Friday and like a javelina accosting a trash bin on the Saturdays and Sundays. I ate a sandwich bag full of fruit that usually consisted of sliced apples, pineapples, and strawberries coupled with a cup of green tea leaves with pomegranate and ginger root for breakfast. Lunch was a small portion of grilled chicken, a handful of raw spinach, grape tomatoes and a chopped carrot that usually invoked coworkers say stuff like, "man, you look like you're feeding a tortoise" and I'd reply, "yeah, the tortoise won the race." As a snack, I'd have a banana and a couple handfuls of raw, mixed nuts and seeds. For dinner, I'd eat oatmeal with coconut oil, honey, cinnamon, raisins, and blueberries.

This eating routine was stuck to with the essence of glue for at least ten months. I can't count how many times friends questioned that I was afraid and/ or paranoid of contracting Covid because I refused time and again to join them out to eat pizza and sushi for dinner but rather, I was adhering to a commitment. Weekends welcomed my cathartic gluttony. I meditated for fifteen minutes every morning when I woke up. I did the same every night before I went to sleep. Like any effective alchemist, I started cleaning out thoughts in my mind camouflaged as worry that didn't serve me, and in turn manipulated them into intentions to manifest and serve me well.

It works. REALLY WORKS. I was reading a book a week. Then I bought a new laptop and started compiling scrolls of writing I'd written to publish my own books. A pair of hiking boots was purchased online when I found a deal, then I was gifted by an accidental, extra pair when they were delivered. I was set as I then started ripping through terrain throughout the southwest and taking road trips when I wasn't working. I started taking supplemental vitamins in my late teens, but now I was also an herbal remedy disciple with a regiment of sea moss, black seed oil, elderberry, milk thistle, sea buckthorn and soursop.

I refused to watch the news at all. I started deleting and unfollowing people on my social media by the hundreds if I determined all they posted was negative poppycock, because that was the only avenue, I was using for overall world information besides my own separate research.

I seldom watch TV, but I got sucked in by Netflix, watching documentaries and movies. While everyone was watching Tiger King and The Last Dance, I kept three movies in heavy rotation that always stayed on during the day even when I wasn't home- The Shawshank Redemption (my all-time favorite movie), The Curious Case of Benjamin Button (my second) and Eternal Sunshine of the Spotless Mind (the oddest love story that still fascinates me). Having these on at all times allowed to do other things without wasting time by sitting and watching. I can recite the dialogue of those movies verbatim and backwards. I did eventually sit down to watch The Last Dance and thoroughly enjoyed it as a lifetime hooper. Tiger King had my attention for about ten minutes of the first episode before my brain cells formed a committee and questioned what I was doing with my life.

Another thing I did was take to financial literacy with a voracious appetite of better understanding. I faithfully listened to podcasts, along with read books on the way to develop better practices of budgeting/saving, creating multiple streams of income, and familiarizing myself with the stock market. Particularly in the areas of index funds and ETFs through companies like Vanguard. I realized passive income is the ultimate weapon of the wealthy and I was at the perfect juncture of my life to explore such options being single without children yet. Scrutinizing numbers in terms of finances changes everything. It made me look at relationships differently, who I wanted to consider partnering with to start a family. Speaking of partnership, that's the objective- to form a partnership, not a sponsorship- in the words of Shannon Sharpe. I bought a brand-new car and kept my clunker to drive on weekends for Uber Eats (a sheer gold mine when the country shut down).

Like my eating habits, this was another area that perplexed my friends because I was always unavailable on the weekends without an explanation because I kept my enterprise close to the vest (sorry Mike, the cat is out of the bag now, but I assure you they won't outwork us). I'm not boasting, but that stream of income gave me $400 dollars extra weekly that stacked then flipped into purchasing vending machines later for another avenue of income. The laws of nature govern the animal kingdom where survival is determined largely by who you choose to surround yourself with, and I started to examine my inner circle differently. Run as fast as the gazelle to escape being food for the lion or run as fast as the lion to make the gazelle its food. The packs you run in are imperative to the outcomes. I don't have an undefeated playbook nor am I muscling through this with a mastered sense of knowing but, mastering habits do contribute to favorable outcomes.

Also, respect due and peace to those who have been afflicted firsthand by the pandemic or lost loved ones. You are not discounted, overlooked, or forgotten here and I'm not exempt of the tides of devastation that have stretched out and touched everyone in some capacity. Most importantly, the pandemic became an inescapable opportunity to embrace our mortality as the horror of it became ubiquitous. For me, fear and everything attached to fear became my friend, because fear understood is as essential as water for survival. I cherish my loved ones more. The value of time is heightened, and anyone who wastes their time no longer has access to mine because it's obvious they haven't caught the lesson of this elongated ordeal. I usually phrase "love is the panacea" as the motif of my writing but two years into a pandemic has bestowed upon me the epiphany that adaptation is the new panacea because what we have endured, and what we know as a pandemic is really one disguised as life. A microcosm I doubt many of us imagined we'd encounter.

On a side note, and along with my homeboy mentioned earlier who is serving a bid in prison, I'd like to express my genuine appreciation to a couple unsung guides for me throughout the pandemic. Chris Duren, the sixteen-year-old little brother from the YMCA who looks up to me and would send videos of himself tirelessly working on dribbling drills outside his house in the scorching heat during the summer daily while I was feeling robbed about not being able to go to the gym to play basketball for the first time in my life. You destroyed my excuses and illustrated resilience. And Bowser, the dog who cared about nothing other than seeing me return home every day with gargantuan smile and a wildly wagging tail. You were the sensei who gave me solace while the world was crumbling like a cookie in a vice grip.

What my dad taught me about the true meaning of fatherhood.

Delano Price has accomplished many things thus far in his life. He is a transformative figure in his community that spans many demographics of people who will readily corroborate his contributing deeds and feats that have been deservingly highlighted. In 2011, he was inducted into the Pima County Sports Hall of Fame where he was also hired as a consultant to the Pima County Office of Education. Researching and collecting data on this county's after school child care programs, to determine areas in need of improvement for future decisions regarding the direction of programs and funding.

He is a former basketball All-American and captain of Tucson High's last state championship team of

1969. He went on to become an All-Conference player at Phoenix Community College, before returning to Tucson to earn undergraduate and graduate degrees at the University of Arizona. He became Tucson's first black coach for boys' varsity basketball at Sunnyside High School, and first black administrator at Sahuaro High School, while going on to serve as one of the most dynamic and respected leaders as a coach, teacher, and administrator in the Sunnyside and Tucson Unified School Districts over thirty-three years. Watching him connect with people is a witnessed artform because he has an innate ability to intuitively navigate the nuances of each person's personality individually and en masse, which is displayed when he gives impromptu speeches as a gifted orator. These are some of the adornments on his resume but, his biggest achievement to me has been as a father.

When I was around six years old, I got a brand-new BMX bike. I was instantaneously attached to and territorial of the shiny blue bike. So much so, that I parked it inside of the house in my room for the first month. One afternoon, I rode it around the neighborhood and happened to meet two kids at the end of Genova, the street we lived on. They were brothers, one being eight and the other eleven. I quickly befriended them, and we rode our bikes around for a couple of hours until our encounter soured when one of them demanded that I give them my bike. When I refused, they both shoved me to the ground and rode off laughing. Where they erred is that they allowed me to see the house they lived in when they rode into the front yard.

Normally, my weapon of choice was rocks with bigger kids for physical leverage but that afternoon, I discovered that my biggest rock was my father. I got up and rode my bike home. When I walked into the bathroom where I found my father shaving, I told him what happened. He put the razor down and told me to show him where the kids lived, and we proceeded to walk down the street together.

If nostalgia could produce its own laughter, it's howling now as I write this because I'll never forget the reaction those kids' father had when he opened the door after we rang their doorbell. My father was standing there with a face full of Barbasol foam, a Jheri curl, sweatpants, and his shirt off! He has always been in premium shape, but this was a zenith condition that rivaled Apollo Creed from the movie Rocky as he was playing basketball and lifting weights religiously at that time. If "nan nanny boo-boo" had a countenance, I personified it when those kids were made to apologize to me by their father. I rode my bike several times by their house after that day, but never saw them come out again.

My father is a man of action. He didn't wait to clean his face off and put on a shirt on that day. Although that's one of my favorite anecdotes to give as an example for my father from a protective standpoint, my sisters can attest with their own stories. Like the time my oldest sister was being bullied by a jealous family in high school and my father walked into their living room and said, "this stops today" in more of a form of an expletive diatribe. It stopped that day. He did the same for my other sister when a kid hurled a racial epithet at her. That time, the kid had a father the neighborhood feared, but my father went into that house as well. Nary a racial slur was hurled at my sister again after he walked out. I never collected comic books as a kid because days were pages turned in the life of my real live superhero.

I didn't need to read statistics throughout adolescence to know that children without fathers were at the greatest detriment. Nor that a staggering number of absentee black fathers had disavowed their sons in the 90's, after the devastation of the crack epidemic ravaged our communities like a tidal wave during the 80's. All I had to do was look around my social milieu or hang with my boys long enough to see that their fathers had either willingly vanished or were reluctant to show up to begin with. Any fool can get a woman pregnant, but it takes a man to execute his responsibilities as a father.

My father gave me his time. He took me to the barbershop every other Friday. He told my second-grade teacher that he wouldn't allow her to label me as "aggressive" after I had punched a classmate for bothering me. My father knew those type of labels are connotative tags a black boy wears on the school-to-prison pipeline. I saw my father when I woke up every morning. I saw my father when he would get home, flip his tie over his shoulder and start preparing dinner.

My father woke me and my sisters up to clean the house on Saturday mornings; the blaring signal was usually "Early in the Morning" by the Gap Band, "All night long" by Mary Jane Girls, or "Don't Look Any Further" by Dennis Edwards. My father did yardwork on Sundays and cut the grass with a push mower (still does). My father made sure if I could recite rap lyrics line for line, I could also recite history lessons date for date. My friends saw my father become their father figure by proximity of our friendship because most of them were fatherless. My father taught me how to invest by being with his greatest asset, my mother. I learned that health is wealth through my father watching him maintain a workout regimen and eat healthy foods since before I can remember.

My father is my best friend. Like a backcourt mate with a chemistry, we share that looks like seamless pick and rolls, back door cuts and passes placed in shooting pockets from adept skill. When I was a kid, they told me that man was created in God's image. Innocent of what blasphemy was my understanding at the time was that my father was that image. That's how much I revered my father and still do. My father once told me that being a black man is demanding. Thank God part of my wealth has been to have a father like mine as an example.

Letter to Frair: Expressing gratitude for a lifetime of love.

My quintessential mother. She is a heart person, with esoteric usage of altruism. She served as the portal for me to come here, her image is the only one that will ever be inked on my skin.

Frair, do you remember these words from my Amazon bestselling debut book, "My Train Is on Schedule" that served as an ode to the woman I call "Frair?" YOU! Your mother was nicknamed "Frair" and at some point, as a kid when I heard the nickname, I started to playfully refer to you by the name because I liked the phonetics of it, and it felt uniquely endearing. You have been my biggest fan and supporter of my writing since the first time my dominant hand moved from left to right, smearing lead across the margins of a moleskin.

Isn't your mother supposed to be your biggest fan? Maybe, but I'd be hard pressed to find anyone who could match your tireless persuasion of me to publish my writing. Way before others told me that I had a gift- leaving newspaper clippings and articles on my bed, or on the kitchen table at the house when I'd visit during college. Fate conspired in my favor being born to a cheerleader- the first black cheerleader at The University of Arizona in the 70's, which is celebrated and corroborated by articles in "The USA Today" (1998), and The Arizona Daily Star (2022). "A society is as free as the black women within it," and you've been a groundswell of opposition to oppression back to the days you wore an Afro the circumference of Angela Davis'. What an honor!

Your modesty won't allow you to enter the terrain of self-aggrandizement, but I'll gladly summon the spirit of Miles Davis with a "So What" in trumpeting your accomplishments. Not just as a mother, but as a person, I've only ever seen you exemplify honesty and integrity. Quintessential. You reject scuttlebutt, and if someone seeks your confidentiality, it's indelibly engraved into concrete secrecy. The same pertains to the gratitude I have for you so; I'm taking this opportunity highlight a few of the innumerable moments I'd like to give thanks for.

Only a heart person can illustrate your esoteric usage of altruism. A resplendent star within your own space, you sacrificed so that your husband could finish college, while you worked after giving birth to Tanisha Nicole Price. You and your high school sweetheart were at the tender age of twenty. You were a sophomore pioneer with pom poms and kicks higher than your aspirations of going to Law school after finishing your bachelor's degree. You lovingly got married while nourishing the inception of a family that would channel Adrian Anitra Price five years later, and Marquez Delano Price a decade later. Only a small number of people with a specialized knowledge or interest can understand that. Esoteric.

At eighteen, you were captain of the cheerleading team while simultaneously the coveted prom queen. At sixteen, you and your brother who was fourteen, were driving a city away to visit your mother who had fallen ill. She passed when you were nineteen, a loss that inevitably became a gaping hole in your brother's heart too insurmountable to prevail. You continued to take care of your little brother through the throes of woe within his life and then nursed your father until he was two months shy of 100 years old. Again. Esoteric. That garners repetitive emphasis. Your capacious storage for altruism is saintly.

You've been doggedly loyal your husband and like a consummate mother with compassion, you've been doggedly loyal to each one of your children even during circumstances that merit taking a position with one of the four immediate family members which you vehemently abstain from. You weigh matters in the depths of love that all of us combined have yet to cultivate because you were doing it long before the four of us entered your life. I once heard that a woman would do what's necessary for her survival when you're in a partnership with her, but a mother will do what's necessary for your survival. To me, my mother can execute each role as a woman and mother equally proficiently.

How many community organizations are you involved in? How many quarrels have you served as an intermediary for? Your stalwart involvement in church. You're devout in your belief system, but it's not so much your devotion to that system, but rather your commitment to being a paragon in orchestration of how your moral compass navigates through interactions with everyone. This is how I determine how authentic or faux someone is when they attempt to proselytize their gospel to me. I got my compassion from you. I learned how to love from you. Your capacity to hold space for others- taking phone calls from family members and friends into the wee hours of the morning offering counseling. "Nana" as your grandchildren call you, have seen you swoop in countless times to create sanctuary as well.

I remember you made this basket of fried chicken for me when I was away playing basketball in college. I ate all eleven pieces in two days! One of my teammates came to my studio apartment and I offered him some the last piece as I was about to devour it. When he bit into it, he said, "You make this!? This is bomb!" I told him that I made it as my gluttony ate up his compliments along with the previous eleven pieces! I did the same thing years later when you made me two sweet potato pies, and I offered one to a couple I know. When they called me extolling the delightful delicacy, I took culinary credit again. One recipe I can never take credit for is your sweet collard greens. Collard greens aren't usually sweet, but that's how you make them, and everyone who eats them is subsequently hooked by and tortured by incessant hankerings for more.

That same motif of sweetness is displayed when I talk to you on the phone every day and you thank me for calling you. That perplexes me because I can't imagine not showing my gratitude by hearing your voice every day. You walk me to my car after every visit and have me text you when I get home to make sure I'm home safe. You got me every Teenage Mutant Ninja Turtle figurine created when I was a kid but were firm in taking my game console away during the school week. I could only get it back after I turned in a signed weekly progress report from school.

Thank you for serving as the portal to bring me here, Frair. You need to you that your love continues to leave an indelible mark on me. It's made me a good man. Your image is the only one that will ever be inked on my skin.

IN THE SHADOWS OF PERCEPTION: ESSAYS ON BEING AN OBSERVER

Digital Detox: A week without screens and what I discovered.

I had a paradoxical epiphany recently while I was holding and looking at the screen of my Android. In the age of technology where almost anything can be accessed by the kiss of a fingertip and a touchscreen, I started to contemplate what negative effects of screen time could I ascertain through a week of digital detox. Digital detox is known as a period during which one refrains from using electronic devices such as computers or smartphones and is regarded as an opportunity to reduce focus or stress on social interaction in the physical world. Society's dependence on digital devices has increased substantially in recent years. From laptops and smartphones to smart appliances and wearable technology, these devices have become essential and ubiquitous parts of daily life. They facilitate communication, entertainment, health management, shopping, and work amongst others. Nevertheless, this dependence also elevates perturbation about cybersecurity, privacy, and the digital divide. As technology resumes advancement, society's reliance on digital devices is likely to enlarge further, sculping how we interact with the world as we know it. I wondered if being bereft of technological advantages would make me feel prehistorically inept when I rendered my phone to a mere land line—eschewing all apps and cheat codes afforded by the bells and whistles of a smartphone that facilitate the simplest daily tasks.

The impact of digital overload.

The first thing I noticed during my digital detox was decreased stress and anxiety. Being devoid of the numerous pings that incessantly intrude my peace was refreshing. As a writer, the constant exposure to emails, notifications, and social media have led to heightened stress levels and anxiety as I've inevitably felt the pressure to stay connected and respond promptly to everyone. Aside from some of the duties I monetarily delegate to my willing girlfriend, I'm a one-man team. I had to mute the vibration on my phone because the uncomfortable alarm of ping after ping was becoming visceral. When I was a kid, my mother was all about following through. I remember after a birthday party where I had amassed an ungodly number of toys as gifts from friends, my mother sat me at the table the next day to write a thank you card to each person who had given me a gift. For some reason, that left an indelible mark on me (She trained me well) and is inextricably and oddly connected to my need to respond to every notification I receive. If I post something on Facebook and garner one-hundred comments, one-hundred responses usually ensue. I recently abandoned that extreme approach to follow through, and I have placed more boundaries. Instead of responding right away, I give myself a window of forty-eight hours to respond. It has irrefutably alleviated anxiety and stress.

To piggyback off being a one-man team with the angelic aid of my girlfriend, my attention span increased during my digital detox. It goes without saying that overindulgent screen time can hinder attention span and concentration, making it difficult to focus on tasks, and leading to decreased productivity. From a delayed eureka moment, I realized how annoying it must have been when I was spending time with my girlfriend, and she looked over to see me checking my Instagram notifications or text messages to service the needs of others before ours as partners. Detoxing digitally has helped me realign healthily with her primarily, as well as others in situations where technology decimates intimate interaction. It has helped me zero in closer through the lens of appreciation when I see my parents on the weekends, beholding the bestowed blessings of still having them both. I laugh a little harder when a friend cracks a joke, amplifying group guffaws during gatherings. My girlfriend reciprocates with the same sensory perception I am grateful for. Overall, I feel better and reconnected. Digital connection creates the illusion of connection, and I can see how excessive reliance on digital communication can lead to feelings of isolation and social withdraw, especially when face-to-face interactions are neglected. To address these issues, I think it's crucial to prioritize face-to-face interactions, establish distinct boundaries for digital usage, work at active listening and empathy in digital communication, and nurture a healthy balance between online and offline interactions.

Benefits of digital detox.

I feel that taking a break from digital devices can lead to an upgraded mental well-being by reducing stress, improving sleep quality, stimulating better interpersonal connections, and contributing to mindfulness. Disconnecting from screens allows individuals to engage in activities that boost relaxation, creativity, and physical activity, which are vital for overall mental health.

Addressing challenges.

I thought of ways to overcome the resistance to disconnecting during my digital detox. One way was to communicate my intentions. I explained to friends and family why I was disconnecting and asked for their support. Technological devices have spiked sensitivity because instant gratification has emboldened our sense of privilege towards those who we expect to be always readily available. Most of us know someone who preemptively send incessant messages if they consider our response to their text not tended to fast enough. I haven't done well with those type of people in the past as I normally ignore their messages until I feel like replying, but I've learned that they may be more understanding and respectful of my need for digital detox if they know my reasons.

Beginning with short periods of disconnection, starting small can gradually increase the duration as you become more comfortable with it. A moderate approach can help ease the transition and minimize anxiety about being offline. I liken this to a crash diet. They're temporarily successful, but permanently create dizzying obstacles against establishing the consistency that merits healthy living. Going cold turkey hadn't worked for me in the past. This time around, I took calculated steps towards weaning off technological allure. Identifying enjoyable offline activities to fill the time usually spent on digital devices, such as reading, exercising, spending time outdoors, or engaging in hobbies is also helpful. For me, reading, exercising, and spending time outdoors were very effective. My method was simple. Every time I had the urge to become engrossed by a device, I'd peel open a small book that carried around and read a paragraph. After a few times, I developed the habit of going straight to my book when a notification sound attempted to render me to a Pavlov reaction. My rule for detaching from devices when I exercise is to leave anything with a screen in my car or a visible corner of the facility I'm working out in and in nature, it's an abomination to be technologically preoccupied in precious juxtaposition to the elements. I also learned to take advantage of apps and settings on my devices to limit screen time. Blocking distracting websites and notifications helped support my commitment to disconnecting as well.

Counterarguments.

There are a few arguments when addressing potential objections to digital detox. One is the dependency argument where some have argued that digital devices are necessary for communication, staying informed and work, making it difficult to disconnect. With communication, a chasm appears to have been generationally wedged between those who experienced life before it was a requirement to be technologically inclined, and those I refer to as "screen babies," people who were born to a word where a device was attached to them right after their umbilical cord was severed. How can someone who adheres to a landline communicate with someone who is more comfortable speaking primarily through text volleys? I've seen the gap bridged by my nieces and nephew when they call my mother. The solution that remedies their disparate ways of communicating has been through facetime. They call each other several times throughout the day which means they see each other a few times a day. They also catch my mother up to speed new device developments which is pretty gratifying for both sides. I remember getting text messages from my father for the first time a few years ago with acronyms like "LOL." It blew my mind in the sense that he is just fine with being a technological dinosaur. I think both my parents, and my nieces and nephew, allow me to balance my view of technology with perspective clarity.

Productivity concerns is another argument that critics might point out that cutting off digital access could hinder productivity largely in professions reliant on technology.

Some might worry that a digital detox could isolate them from friends, family, and online communities, especially in a world where virtual connections are growingly important. Here, I think this affects adolescents and introverts to a large extent. Being that this generation of teenagers have grown up accustomed to technological devices, weaning off may hinder navigation within social milieus. Being an ambivert myself, there are times when I like to interact with others face-to-face, while other times, a screen or nothing at all suites me the same way.

Digital platforms provide a plethora of entertainment and information, and some might argue that a digital detox could lead to missing out on treasured content or opportunities. During 2020 when the Covid19 pandemic arose, I remember deactivating my Facebook account. It lasted for all of forty-eight hours when I realized that most of entertainment and information, I was taking in was through that social media platform. For instance, I learned about a book by Noam Chomsky after a friend posted it. That post led me to various works by Chomsky. I also attended two of his lectures subsequently. When my parents grew up, the news aired invariably at set times. Today, media is available through a twenty-four-hour conveyor belt of information. If you don't watch the news, and you disregard most digital platforms, it's not easy to stay informed unless you are a student of life that goes to the library, reads, and is inclined to research, and study. By and large, that is unfortunately a lost art.

There's a fear of missing out on important events, news, or social interactions that could occur online during the detox period. The contrary is to miss out on the human experience. Is it not peculiar that eye contact has become a relic of nostalgia? Either way, events, news, and social interactions tend to keep us tethered online with trepidation of losing out during periods of detox. I have a penchant of disdain for talking on the phone for the most part, but hearing a voice on the other end of the line feels more welcoming than the endless ways nuances are misconstrued through text messages. Using phone calls to disseminate information pertaining to events, news, or social interactions are just as effective, but I also understand that our overindulgence in external stimuli has pushed options of the like into oblivion.

Other critics might argue that instead of completely detoxing from digital devices, it's better to acquire knowledge of using digital devices and platforms in moderation, encouraging healthier habits without the need for maximal measures.

After a week of digital detox, I would implore anyone to at least try it for a twenty-four to forty-eight hours. I'm an extremist who tends to vacillate, but I hold steadfast in encouraging others to experience the abstinence of their most frequented devices from time to time. I believe the most practical step for implementation is approach it like a fast. When fasting from food, it's ideal to first prepare mentally. Set goals that are clear and understand your intention. The next step is to gradually transition from a regular diet to the reduction of meal sizes leading up to the fast to ease into it. The same would apply to devices, minimizing usage leading up to a detox. Avoiding heavy usage is tantamount to refraining from heavy intake of food. The same would apply to ending the fast or detox—beginning with digestible amounts of usage with gradual reintroduction.

In conclusion, a healthy digital balance has become climacteric in today's interconnected world. By striking a balance between online and offline lives, we can encourage well-being, lift productivity, and nurture meaningful relationships. I think it's better to embrace technology wisely, ensuring it enriches rather than inundates our lives. In seven days, I was able to ascertain that as wonderful as our technological devices are, they are still unable to experience the world through the sensory lens like the sentient beings we are. Hopefully I can stay secure within that notion before acquiescing to the whim of my next device notification.

The art of Minimalism: Simplifying your life for more joy and less stress.

During my documentary binge watching during the pandemic between 2020 and 2021, I came across a documentary on Netflix entitled, "Minimalism: A documentary about the important things" which is an episode compilation of a video-essay series that explores a specific problem spawned by consumerism—from busyness and impulse to social media and destabilization of the economy. I was already aware that minimalism was a lifestyle involving the reduction or simplification of one's material possessions, and in turn, it can potentially free one to lead an existence that is more intentional, purposeful, and spiritual.

Being that I was in the throes of the pandemic like most people, I was relentlessly looking for solutions that would broaden my peace of mind while confined to quarantine. The title of the documentary piqued my interest and the testimonials along with the visual validation of the series seized by undivided attention. Once the documentary ended, I immediately started to take inventory of my abode, scanning every square inch of my space to ascertain what no longer served me. It gave me a sense of control, liberation, and power during a time where solitude was no longer synonymous with sanctuary. The more space I cleared, the more emancipated my overall being felt because of my newfound practices of minimalism. I focused on three practices of minimalism.

Practice 1: Decluttering.

The first practice I adopted was decluttering. I regularly assessed and removed unnecessary possessions to create a simplified living space. Not allowing possessions to possess me, especially if I deemed the possession futile daily. The next part of the process was for me to release the possession by gifting or selling it to someone else I felt could benefit from using it. Heirlooms entrusted to me or things of sentimental value being exceptions, but I took it even further by designating a space where the possession wouldn't clutter or obstruct the flow of my newly discovered feng shui.

This practice conjured reverberations of nostalgia— one of the Cyrano de Bergerac classics— the movie starring Jose Ferrer that I used to watch with my father as a kid. A quote Cyrano made in the movie now visited me with much more clarity when he said that he only "wore his adornments on his soul." I realized further that I've never been one to harbor possessions and from a spiritual standpoint, have always carried my altars and built shrines within me, that allow me to access my ancestors and the source directly no matter where I am. My approach to my possessions or lack thereof now also allowed me to identify with my fascination of how Jay-Z constructs his lyrical lines while recording songs— straight from his mind to melody with his vocals substituting for a pen and pad.

The best way I can impart advice for embracing decluttering is to affirm that first, letting go allows you to declutter. Ater that, the best way to look at possessions is to remain within a space that doesn't allow possessions to possess you.

Everyone is different, but I also believe there's an attainable healthy balance between coexisting with intrinsic things that have sentimental value, and the downhearted stories of that "Hoarders" (TV series) show for everyone that can help them. I think acknowledgement and acceptance, followed by practice, can help anyone get started.

Practice 2: Mindful Consumption.

A. Explanation of mindful consumption B. Contrast between consumerism and mindful consumption C. Strategies for practicing mindful consumption in daily life.

Mindful consumption has been defined as the practice of being consciously aware of how, what, and why you consume goods and services. It involves being intentional in your choices, considering the effects of your consumption on the environment, others, and yourself. This can involve aspects like ethical sourcing, sustainable production, lessening waste, and being present in the moment while consuming. By practicing mindful consumption, individuals orient themselves to a more sustainable and fulfilling lifestyle while minimizing harm to the planet and society.

An interesting way to look at mindful consumption is through the contrast between consumerism and mindful consumption. Both represent contrasting approaches to getting and using goods and services. Consumerism anchors on the continuous acquisition of goods and services, often guided by materialistic desires or societal pressures. It encourages unrestrained buying, often beyond one's needs, leading to overconsumption and resource depletion. It can emphasize instant gratification and short-term satisfaction over long-term sustainability and tends to prioritize quantity and novelty over quality and durability.

During the pandemic, if an item couldn't serve me from day-to-day, I simply disregarded it as an option. This reminded me of a time when my grandfather saw me wear three different pairs of shoes in one week. Him being adamant about only being able to wear one pair at a time instilled in me that shoes are to be worn, not to be coveted. Practicality examined and exercised, gave me greater differentiation of what I wanted and needed.

For some reason, shoes helped me grasp this practice the most because I have friends that have thousands of dollars' worth of shoes in their closest and friends that wear one all-purpose pair of shoes for years before they purchase another. In the past, I've vacillated between both examples. Being mindful of what I bring into my life, focusing on quality and necessity rather than quantity has helped me create space from the gravitational pull of instant gratification.

Extending the examination of mindful consumption further, I recall a time several years ago when I was watching Saul Williams on "The Breakfast Club" speaking ardently on the subject that captivated me as if he was delivering a soliloquy— "because I write rhymes, I write poems, I write songs and basically, I feel like your diet isn't only what you eat. It's what you watch, it's what you read, it's what you listen to, and so I'm mindful of what I ingest, and so basically there was nothing there that was feeding me...it became a matter of me minding my diet." This seeped into my pores of comprehension what I heard his expression on the matter. It's carried me ever since in a way that keeps me intentional and mindful of my mindful consumption. Everything from music to relationships, platonic and romantic were altered substantially.

Practice 3: Simplifying Lifestyle.

Simplifying your lifestyle can involve streamlining your wardrobe, establishing a consistent routine, and committing to minimalism. In terms of wardrobe simplification, declutter your wardrobe by getting rid of items you no longer wear or need and create a capsule wardrobe with versatile, high-quality pieces that can be mixed and matched. You'd be surprised how far a pair of jeans, a t-shirt, a hoodie, and a pair of durable shoes can get you, and if you live in my hometown of Tucson, Arizona, a pair of shorts, a t-shirt, and a pair of durable shoes can span across four seasons with our weather. I try to invest in timeless staples rather than trendy pieces and adopt a "one in, one out" rule to prevent an amassment of unnecessary items.

For routine establishment, I establish a daily routine that includes consequential tasks such as exercise, work/study time, and relaxation. It helps me to prioritize tasks and activities that align with my values and goals. With exercise, it's easy for me to prioritize because I see health as wealth. During another interview, I saw Kevin Gates say that he is selfish when it comes to his personal time working out, and he is unwilling to miss exercise because it affords him the mental clarity and continued intestinal fortitude that he needs first service himself, and then everyone around him who depend on him like his family. That resonated with me.

Simplifying my schedule by avoiding overcommitment and learning to say no when necessary is also helpful. If found that even with loved ones, love can only be mutual when boundaries are put in place because it helps foster respect. Incorporating mindfulness practices such as meditation and journaling to stay grounded and focused are accommodating ways to chart cultivation.

By simplifying your wardrobe, establishing a routine that aligns with your priorities, and committing to minimalism, you can create a more intentional and fulfilling lifestyle.

After practicing minimalism, myself over a duration of time, my call to action is simple—welcome simplicity and declutter your life with minimalism. Start by assessing your possessions, focusing on what accurately adds value. Simplify your routines, prioritize experiences over things, and cultivate a more mindful and intentional lifestyle. The minimalist movement facilitates a more fulfilling and meaningful existence.

Heights: How my only fear took me higher.

I have an ambivalent relationship with heights. I prefer the window seat when traveling on airplanes for views. The thrill of roller coasters has rendered me to a gravitational pull, attracting me to Six Flags every few years for a day of exhilaration. In contrast, if I stand atop a table, I'm woozy; and you'll never see me walk along the edge of the second floor or higher of a mall because I have a fear that someone, anyone will push me off. (Somebody betrayed me in another lifetime!) I figured out that I'm the person who will readily tightrope walk, but there better be a safety net underneath me or else my fear of heights will otherwise thwart any such attempt to chance an imminent fall. It's called Acrophobia, a nemesis of my psyche.

I discovered my fear of heights on my first hike with some friends from my neighborhood when I was around seven years old. We got a ride out of the city and into the desert from an older brother of one of my friends who also served as our guide that day. I saw my first rattlesnake that we agitated with sticks and rocks from foolhardy range; its blood-curdling rattle only activated more of our inept experience posturing with potential danger. We slap boxed and exchanged incessant banter with no aid of water for hydration on what was probably a triple digit summer day. Traversing the desert terrain into what seemed like an upward spiraling staircase along the side of a mountain is where things got real for me. The path narrowed to where our backs were against the mountain and the tips of our toes neared the edge as we sidestepped along the way. At that point, I looked down and focused on the one-hundred-foot drop and stopped moving. What I felt, I imagined the fly feels when it stares into the eyes of the spider approaching it while stuck on its web. It took an hour for them to coax me to finally move, and I only moved because they had to pass me to retrace our steps to exit the mountain.

A year later, my family moved to one end of the desert in the city, and I unearthed two things about myself that would later solidify as what will be lifetime companions without knowing it upon inception: hiking and meditation. There were no other kids in the neighborhood, so I spent a lot of time wandering in the desert by myself. I called it "exploring" and found along the way that although I was very social and had a lot of friends at school, I was also comfortable alone. This alone time heightened my senses, seeing mica in the sand and smelling creosote from plants. I had no idea until later that I was hiking and meditating in nature.

Other kids soon moved into the area. They joined me in the desert, but basketball leagues soon took me away as my love for basketball directed me to an inordinate number of hours in the gym. In 2009, I got into a relationship with a girl who would help me return to and introduce a new world of hiking as she lived on the opposite side of the desert where I grew up. The hikes she took me to, I had no idea existed in the city. I researched more uncharted territory throughout the mountains to reciprocate in gratitude for additional shared hikes. Basketball remained my first love, but hiking was frequented as I could connect with nature and the kid within me. Fast forward to 2020 when all gyms were shut down, rims from outside courts were removed and this is where the story begins.

Cathedral Rock Sedona, Arizona March 9th, 2021, 4:45am.

I set my alarm for 5:30am but excitement awakened me by 4:45am. Since March 2020 when everything started shutting down, I was hiking daily in Tucson, Arizona after being completely without basketball for the first time in my life. Seven Falls Trail, Sutherland Trail, Romero Pools Trail, Valley View Overlook Trail, Tumamoc Hill Trail, Freeman Homestead Nature Trail, Yetman Trail, Linda Vista Trail, Tanque Verde Falls Trail, Blackett's Ridge Trail, Cactus Forrest Trail, Mount Wrightson via Old Baldy Trail Summit, and Picacho Peak Summit were my baker's dozen. With Tumamoc Monday through Friday mornings, and the other twelve rotating on Saturdays and Sundays. Seventy percent of the time, I went alone. Ten percent was being a guide for my sister and niece on big adventure hikes. Ten percent were dare devil missions that involved rock climbing like Picacho Peak or highest elevation points like Mount Wrightson with a friend of mine who is a high-level hiker. The remaining ten percent, I'd take people who caught wind of my commitment to hiking. I was reticent to surrender most of the time because these hikes gave me sacred time alone, away from the burgeoning madness of the world. Months later, all ground was covered in Tucson, so I started taking road trips within the four corner states of Arizona, Utah, New Mexico, and Colorado seeking more hikes.

March 9th was the first morning of several I'd planned to do in Sedona, Arizona hiking the likes of Doe Mountain, Soldier's Trail, Devil's Bridge, and Bell Rock. I'd researched that Cathedral Rock was a short, favored path up a steep slickrock hillside to the base of a sheer-sided butte, yielding breathtaking views. What I didn't know is that the images I saw online were deceptive. Cathedral Rock is a short but highly technical hike. I started out climbing up a sandy slope past trees and bushes with an arrogant smirk on my face, somewhat feeling disrespected by the ease. As the vegetation started to fade, I started to get a clear look at the surroundings with majestic red rock everywhere.

At this point I swallowed my smirk as I approached the infamously steep slickrock ascent. Two teenage girls and a woman in her sixties arrived simultaneously with me. It was evident that we all shared trepidation now. After a few minutes of silently measuring each other's fear, one of the teenage girls blurted, "welp,

I'm going up" and disappeared, leaving the other teenager mortified. Soon, she went up too. I turned to the woman, and she said she was fine with turning around. Before she did, she told me there was a man with a tan hat who was helping people near the more difficult parts. I heard her but wasn't listening because I was too busy tussling internally with my competitiveness and the disappointing alternative of giving up. I grumbled "hell nah" and started climbing the steep ascent. There are small foot holes, but most of the scale up this section necessitates jamming your feet into crevices and doing a semi-form of rock climbing. I found myself soon wedged between a vertical gully with my nemesis heights, and an unexpected helping hand about to appear like voila.

As I looked back and beneath me and got that same feeling I had stuck on the pathway of that mountain as a kid. I froze up once again, people were gathering at the base of the ascent seemingly waiting for me to fall. Out of nowhere, I heard someone say, "hey buddy...you're okay, I'll coach you through this." Without looking, I responded, "nah dawg, I'm turning around" which is impractical because there's no way but up to go from that point. It's an odd twenty to thirty meters of scrambling vertically where it's physically impossible to backtrack into those crevices and foot holes. I finally looked up and this guy was somehow kneeling diagonally with his heels secured in crevices effortlessly like a Shaolin monk on the branch of a tree. He was smiling and I was able to intuit that he was genuinely a helpful person. I squinted. TAN HAT! This was the guy that woman told me about earlier. "Goat man" as I named him, advised me how to make it the rest of the way. I can't remember his exact instructions. I do know that he told me that the rock I was pressed against was like sandpaper and if I felt like I was going to slip, all I needed to do was lay flat against the rock and it would stymie the slippage. His tutelage was gold.

After we finished, I thanked Goat Man a few hundred times. I was just glad to be standing flat foot with a surface underneath me again. From there, I continued for 0.5 miles of moderate and steep hiking that is comparable to climbing a football stadium. The views at the top of Cathedral Rock are some of the most captivating in Sedona (or anywhere else) and is the perfect place to be during sunrise which I was gifted by the highest that morning. The most popular spot is at the end of the trailhead, where a ledge drops down and faces the horizon. I met Goat Man's wife and daughter, taking a picture with him because I had to remember this guy and somehow, I knew I'd tell this story one day. There were many other people at the top, but the canyon felt like I was seated at the bottom of a Tibetan singing bowl, offering an unmatched quietude and stillness. I pulled out some written intentions, read them silently to myself and meditated for about thirty minutes, occasionally slivering my eye lids open to behold the picturesque scenery.

When I opened my eyes fully, a couple walked up to me and asked if I could take a picture of them to which I did then asked them to do the same for me. Their names were Faisal and Laura. They were visiting from Louisiana. We returned to the bottom together, exchanged information and met for sushi that night. Turned out I made such a spectacle being wedged in that gully that Laura took a picture of me and Goat Man before meeting me at the top because she was unsure if she'd be able to climb the ascent. The picture is framed in my office. I've stayed in contact with them, and they just returned to Sedona recently to get married. Cathedral Rock isn't that difficult for the average hiker but throw in the fear of heights combined with that vertical gully and you've got yourself a formidable challenge.

For that moment, that felt like an eternity when the paralysis of fear possessed me, something strange happened before I heard Goat Man speak to me. Most of the time when people find themselves in the throes of a precarious situation with an unknown life or death outcome, they start to bargain with a higher power. "If you help me here, I'll never do" and so on. My experience was oddly different in that I started to bargain with the internal last vestiges of my disappointment, resentment, anger, expectation, and fear accumulated throughout my life. At that point, I decided to let them go because when ascending greater heights, those type of things only prevent you from seeing horizons awaiting your arrival. I wasn't finished facing heights and several months later, I found myself challenging my nemesis in Southwest Utah at Angel's Landing in Zion National Park.

More Heights: How my only fear took me higher. Again.

Angels Landing. Zion National Park. Southwest, Utah. September 28th, 2021. 5:30am.

By and large, black men are uncomfortable in predominately white settings where we know we are outnumbered in a place we are seldom seen. It's something inextricably braided into our DNA going back to our inception of slavery being invaded by colonizers. The mechanism developed as survival over the span of more than 400 years is still embedded indelibly in our collective psyche. Mine was wreaking havoc this morning in Utah where the black population sits at a whopping 1.19%. The stage was set for one of the most interesting days I've ever experienced while on a death-defying hike.

It was an early pitch-dark morning. I only heard voices coming from silhouettes of people as I ambled closer from the parking lot, still half asleep. You must get to the park shuttle early to hike Angels Landing because it's the glamourized "bucket list" hike. In Zion National Park, it ramps up to crowds to the point of being problematic, especially by mid-morning on weekends and holidays during tourist season. There is a consensus that Angels Landing possesses one of the most stunning viewpoints you can experience but, it is not recommended for anyone with a fear of heights (Here, I went again on my own). I was early enough to catch the first shuttle as the sun started to rise.

There were about fifty people ahead of me in a line snaking around barriers and dividers sectioning everyone off into lines. I could also see that I was the only black person there and immediately felt a visceral paranoia, accompanied by a thought that ties back to my opening paragraph. "This had to be how it felt at a slave auction" resounded in my skull in response to the unfettered looks I was getting from all directions of my surroundings that were carried with laser curiosity as to why I was there. The feeling felt tantamount to how the roach must feel when its captor discovers it after the lights are turned on- unwelcome and vulnerable to the whim of its potential captor. The chances of me being harmed by a potential captor was closer to nil than slim, but I need to convey how rooted this is in our DNA. What transpired next is where I believe much of our common human understanding recedes and the universe speaks an esoteric language that flickers like portals you can only enter if willing to converse with it for moments in time.

I'm a keen observer, but how this happened is still beyond the laws of physics to me. Nobody was within a few feet of me (social distancing) when I looked to my left and then swiveled back to my right. I saw a guy standing right next to me, shoulder to shoulder. He was a white guy in his thirties at the time like me. I gave him a precautionary scan to size him up because he seemingly appeared out of thin air. His appearance presented the juxtaposition of a clean-cut TV personality with salon beard/haircut trims; and rugged hiker with hiking boots/backpack, two arm sleeve tattoos, one leg sleeve tattoo and a hockey player's build.

He spoke. "What's up, man?" I replied with a cold, "what up?" The eyes never lie, and I could tell this guy could see how guarded I was through the hesitancy in his eyes. My discernment determined no intended threat. The shuttle branches off into various hikes in the canyon, so he asked, "which hike are you going to hit? I'm taking Angels Landing on first." I told him I was going to Angels Landing first also. Acquainting rapidly, we talked about where we were from, eerily similar tastes in Hip-Hop music, travel, and Tom Brady. His name was Winsor from Boston, Massachusetts and we would remain inseparable for the rest of the day.

Boarding the shuttle, we stood next to the door on the ride to Grotto Trailhead where Angels Landing starts to be the first ones to be let out for a head start. We were naturally laughing and talking about various topics when a group of women in their mid-twenties asked where we were from and if we'd come on the trip to Utah together. I said, "Nah, I just met this dude forty-five minutes ago, where are ya'll from?" The group of CrossFit athletes from Milwaukee, Wisconsin thought our response about meeting each other was facetious which turned into banter on both sides for the rest of the ride. We got separated from them about halfway through the hike, but they left an impression with their competitive and frolic nature as we pushed each other physically starting out the hike.

Angels Landing takes between 3-6 hours to hike. The crowds (attracts 4.3 million visitors a year), steep sandstone steps and potential weather that can be volatile can present a precarious outing. There have also been double digits deaths from falls since the 90's and you must now get a permit to hike Angels Landing. The first section is grueling. You climb about 1,000 feet in elevation over 2 miles to get to the final half-mile ascent that gets much of the attention. The first 1.5 miles is a continuous climb over mostly terrain bereft of shade before you reach "Refrigerator Canyon" which is a brief shady section. I had been hiking incessantly for the past year, so I was fine here. Winsor was in optimum condition as he was step-for-step with me and was able to continue our ongoing conversation about everything (If you ever want to fully gauge someone's physical condition, go on a taxing hike with them and talk the entire time. Most people render themselves mum to preserve their energy. The views along this section are outstanding and the weather was impeccable that morning. After this section is "Walter's Wiggles," a section of 21 close range switchbacks that steeply climb toward "Scout Lookout."

Scout Lookout concludes the first portion of the hike and starts the second section up the spine to Angels Landing. This is where everyone stops to catch their breath, behold the sweeping views, and evaluate whether they want to continue to the summit. I witnessed many people turn around here. After feeling strong powering up the first section, my muscle was deflated as I set my eyes on the spine. While everyone else was taking pictures, mingling, and feeding trail mix to squirrels, I eased away from the crowd to look closer at the spine of the mountain. My heart plummeted in unison with my imagined body, into the abyss of this monstrosity from a repeating reel in my mind. That stubborn old nemesis, my fear of heights, had returned with a vengeance.

As I started to negotiate my way into backing out, Winsor popped up like a cheap car salesman on a midnight infomercial. "You ready for this, bro!?" He was damn near frothing at the mouth, and my mind commuted words my mouth couldn't utter in response because my heart was still in my socks. Earlier, he told me that it was imperative that he made it to the summit because he was carrying a small urn in his backpack with the ashes of someone close to him. He took off towards and up the spine. I followed with the velocity of tortoise, cautiously making my way up some of the chains bolted into the mountain, guard-rails and carved steps which really provided me with zero relief because you're angling diagonally up the side of a steep mountain with death beckoning drop-offs. Winsor realized he'd gotten a good lead on me and turned around to see where I was. When he spotted me, I yelled out, "go 'head, bro...you got it!" He paused with concern as I shook my head and waved him off.

After Winsor disappeared over the spine, a kerfuffle arose as some impatient hiker was yelling at people to get through pockets of traffic behind me. There was younger woman who was grasping tightly to one of the poles connected to the chains, unable to move due to fright. I offered my hand to help her start to make her way down and off the mountain because although I can be chivalrous, I was also looking for a way off the mountain myself. She took my hand, and we made our way down to the base of the spine. She was from New York and her name was Liza with a contagious sense of humor and gregarious nature.

Her two friends, Brooke and Syd had continued up the spine while she got stuck where I found her. After about 30 minutes of getting acquainted through laughter with levity of how we'd both chickened out of finishing the hike, I decided to try again. I told her maybe I'd run into her later in the canyon and she wished me luck on my decision to make another attempt at climbing. The climb throughout was terrifying and I'd be fraudulent in omitting the pertinent fact that I was overcome by panic innumerable times along the way. The defining moment was crossing one exposed section where I allowed myself to look down on both sides to the canyon below. It was the width of a diving board (no hyperbole here, Google away) The best way I can describe it is to imagine walking a plank over the Grand Canyon. What I felt looking down was ineffable, followed by a moment of clarity so immense that it was almost trance-like-sheer meditation. I was devoid for the first time that I can remember in my life from what I described earlier as being embedded in the psyche of the black man.

No, I'm not deluding myself with a kumbaya epiphany to serve as validation that we can all get along in the world, but I do know that only consciousness was present at that moment and nothing else mattered. It made me think about the time I read about how astronauts, upon returning to earth after being in space with a view of the planet, realized that we are small in the grand scheme of things and our differences are even smaller. After, I scrambled a little further, and located Winsor on the final viewpoint waiting for me. I'm sure that feeling within my psyche will remain, but on Angels Landing, I was able to reach a height that allowed me to see a glimpse of what those astronauts were privileged to see. By meeting this stranger and looking down into that canyon from 1,500 feet above the ground.

On the way down, me and Winsor ran into Liza, Brooke, and Syd, finishing the hike together. I hadn't realized how thick of a Bostonian accent Winsor had all day until these three women started cracking jokes on him, pleading him to repeat words like Cowdah (chowder), ahnt (aunt), bee-uh (beer), kahnt (can't), kah (car), eye-dee-er (idea) then guffawing to no avail. Winsor had some slick punch lines of his own and cracked back, so serendipity gifted us more frolic with more people as we started the morning. We did "the secret hike" and an alternative to Observation Point that allowed us to view the entire canyon, perched atop rock formation from catbird seats. After that, we ate dinner and set our sights on "The Narrows" hike for the following morning. Me and Winsor have stayed in touch and plan to meet up for future hikes in Sedona, Yellowstone National Park, and Yosemite National Park. I try to wake up daily with an optimism that seeks to will the probability of having experiences like that day. Not so much the exhilaration of the hike, but rather taking the chance to experience something new through my psyche, and people.

CHAPTER 3

WITNESSING LIFE: REFLECTIONS FROM THE OBSERVER'S LENS

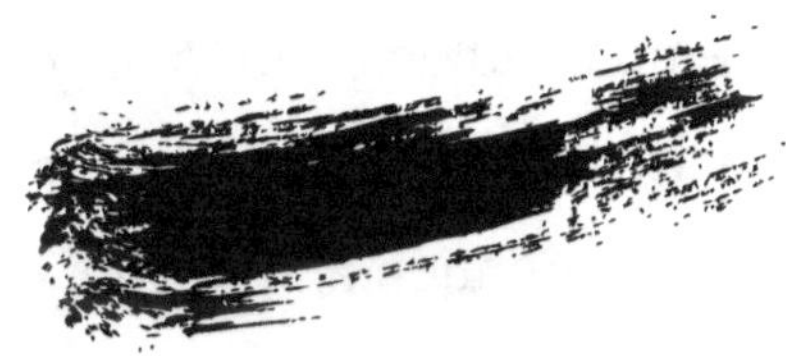

Egypt: My Soul Knows.
A pyramidic experience of a lifetime.

I have spiritual conviction inextricably tied to the pyramids of Cairo, Egypt. As far back as I can remember, pyramidic dreams have permeated my psyche. I started drawing these triangular structures on homework assignments in elementary school that mirrored images in an encyclopedia from the Tolson Elementary school library. Book collecting, incessant study, and obsession leaked into my consciousness until lucid dreams manifested the sound of my feet pitter-pattering atop the same sand where the pyramids stand.

Yet, when I embarked on a trip to Egypt this year in September, it wasn't as grandiose as I had anticipated. The constant consternation and hovering trepidation were seemingly insurmountable at times, but I made it to the pyramids as I believed my vessel was preordained to do so this lifetime. It was meant to be an experience and within that experience, I can now offer my moment of clarity through a chronicled endeavor.

At twenty years old, my girlfriend, who was aware of my prodigious enthrallment with Egypt, gave me a birthday card that read, "Soon you'll be thirty, and we'll be in Egypt together." Thirty came and went. Our relationship ran its course a year and a half later, but the longing to reach those sands in Egypt persisted throughout the corridors where I housed my dream.

When my uncle transitioned to the ancestral plane this past summer, I was told that he had wanted to travel abroad before he passed away, but that hope was curtailed by his last breath. The revelation galvanized me away from exploratory procrastination into booking a flight the next day to Egypt. Amid my vision being tunneled by earnestness to fulfill a prophecy, I omitted to ask my partner if she wanted to join me on the trip. I have a penchant for traveling alone as I did before I met her, but I professed to her, that I periodically longed to travel abroad with a partner that I have a deep connection with. One doesn't have to exhibit romantic prowess to intuit my omission potentially botched the relationship awareness that ensures inclusion in addition to maintaining your word.

She was happy for me, but it was obvious that my brimming enthusiasm was unrequited. Not out of obligation, but rather recall of the initial invitation I extended to her during the genesis of our relationship, I asked her if she'd like to join me. She ardently booked her own flight to join me. We made plans to sit down and research everything that we'd need to know in preparation for the trip, but never made the saved YouTube videos and printed documents a priority that would detail necessitated familiarity with the information. I've never been shy of what some may consider woo-woo, but our haphazard collection notes strewn across my couch started to nudge at my burgeoning apprehension surrounding the trip.

I began to perceive the sudden rise of bickering between us as a premonition, and an article that popped up on my phone broadcasting the arrival of Mercury Retrograde didn't help. Thirty minutes into the flight, we were met with invariable turbulence throughout a grueling nineteen-hour flight. Whether she was a mother or not, my partner is an unparalleled nurturer with a love language of touch. It's second nature for her to soothe others under duress by rubbing their backs, and she can quell a conflagration with her patient kindness. Within that first thirty minutes of the flight when we met turbulence, she was visibly rattled, interlocking her arm with mine, resting her head on my shoulder, while simultaneously rubbing my forearm with her hand. The communicate transference was clear- fear had seized her, and she was ironically soothing herself by attempting to sooth me.

I've never traveled outside of the country with anyone before, let alone a partner, and it was clear that my training as a novice had embarked. The energy transference of fear heightened my awareness of the turbulence. I turned to my partner and said, "Love, we have eighteen more hours of this flight. Turbulence in a plane is akin to experiencing bumps along the road while driving a car. We're alright." When we landed, I can admit that I responded to the grueling flight by immediately becoming engrossed by my phone. Scrolling through social media and answering text messages- leaving my partner to "mother" me through the airport.

Once we got to the shuttle, we were told that we couldn't stay in the same hotel because we are not married, and it is against the customs of Egypt being a Muslim country. Couple that with a woman who deems herself as a W.I.T.C.H (Woman in total control of herself). She was frightened, and despite her outcry not to be separated from me, the plea was muffled. The situation put my masculinity in a quagmire. My visceral reaction was to go Equalizer Robert McCall, but my logic quickly neutralized those delusions of grandeur as I realized our self-assured lack of preparation had caught up to us- ensnared now also by our American hubris thinking we could do as we pleased in another country. As a black man, it brought me closer to the understanding that Africans Americans had to endure slavery and indigenous Africans have had to endure colonization on their own land. I didn't see the moor hued Africans I anticipated.

I wholeheartedly support exploration through travel. I equally implore people who do so to do their research and to stay current on world affairs. After being separated, I caught an Uber to my partner's hotel and brought her to mine. We were slated to board another flight the next morning to Aswan then to Luxor to experience the wonders of antiquity, but my partner was discombobulated, and I was deflated. My empathy was able to affirm and navigate her valid uneasiness, but I was torn- adhering to our decision to forfeit the rest of our scheduled tour out of lost trust from the company, juxtaposed by my underlying disappointment caused by a dream deferred. We recreated our own itinerary during our nine-day stay and made the best of it.

Within that duration, both of us evolved at a maximum Millennium Falcon speed rate through a labyrinth of obstacles in which we prevailed. It made us stronger individually and together in partnership. I'm forever indebted to her because we share a once in a lifetime experience where an odd serendipity manifested her as that travel partner, I longed for.

*My experience was summed up in a
picture taken of me leaping in the air
with the pyramids as the backdrop.
A shemagh as my crown with locs
like lamb's wool manipulating gravity*

underneath. My name and first book across my chest a la hieroglyphs affirming that "My Train is On Schedule." Harem pants parachuted my landing, braced by the Jordan 1's on my feet that made my cypher complete. Through everything that happened, I did what I sought out to do in seeing the pyramids of Giza. One day I'll go back to see the rest. My soul knows.

The Impact of Gratitude: How Cultivating Thankfulness Can Transform Your Life

As a Wu-Tang Clan aficionado, when I contemplate gratitude, it evokes thoughts of a track from their debut album, "Enter the Wu-Tang (36 chambers). The nebulous nostalgia that flashes across the grey matter of my consciousness is the song "Can it be all so simple." As a kid in 1993, I couldn't quite pinpoint the feeling of how that song made me feel—a poetic juxtaposition of hard knock life and coming of age, stitched together by gratitude through the needle of retrospect. I listen to the classic now and the beginning holds more meaning in that the song is now thirty years old— "Hey, you know everybody's talking about the 'good old days.' Everybody! The good old days. Well, let's talk about the good old days." For me, the good old days, and the Wu-Tang Clan both equate to gratitude because they allow me to have readiness in showing appreciation for and to return kindness—there's infinite quality in being thankful. That said, peace to the Gods (RZA, GZA, Method Man, Raekwon, Ghostface Killah, Inspectah Deck, U-God, Masta Killa, Cappadonna, and the late Ol' Dirty Bastard) for bestowing upon myself and all the Wu-afficionados I grew up with a soundtrack to our coming of age.

Practicing gratitude can (as it has done for me) improve mental well-being, foster positive relationships, enhance empathy, and reduce stress. It can shift focus from what's lacking to what's present which promotes overall emotional resilience. My favorite number is seven (also my life path number), so I thought of seven ways of how cultivating thankfulness can transform your life.

Daily Reflection: Take a moment each day to reflect on things you're grateful for, whether big or small. I've found that even on what I've perceived as the worst days, there's always been something to be grateful for. I may have ruined a recipe by burning a meal while preparing it, but the only thing to fret about is the prevalent hunger crisis that seems preposterous in a world where there's enough for everyone to eat if we learn to curb our greed. Big or small, I give thanks. A lot of times, I move through my senses during my daily reflection— giving thanks for sight of the sun even when it shines so bright that my eyes viscerally shut. Giving thanks to the smells of nature remind me to engage with it. Giving thanks for my hearing after listening to the matchless "New Blue Sun" album by André 3000. Giving thanks for the taste of honey after I pour it on mangoes. Giving thanks for touch my lady Fiona, gives me that, has ameliorated my understanding of affection. The more you reflect on what you're grateful for, the more you quell the unnecessary need to find fault in anything else.

Gratitude Journal: Maintain a journal to record positive experiences and express gratitude regularly. I'm a firm believer in writing things down, especially on countless sticky notes in an age of tablet technology. The tangibility of writing something down seems to interlace what I've jotted down into my synapses with the same adhesive on the back of those notes I have a penchant to collect as physical files. Those same things that I reflect on daily, I write down. They serve as Marley mantras that "Everything's gonna be alright." Albeit I tend to record more positive experiences as an incorrigible optimist, I also record negative experiences to "keep it all in perspective," as my father indoctrinated me with early as a boy growing up. I'm grateful for that lesson from my father. When he reads this, I hope he knows that that lesson has been a torch through many tunnels of adversity throughout my life. On behalf of all native sons, we salute our black fathers.

Express Thanks: Verbalize or write down your gratitude towards others, fostering positive connections. I believe that we all are children masquerading as adults, and the best way to enrich a person's sense of self is to offer them gratitude and positive reinforcement. It makes connecting transitionally smooth and builds trust. I've found that even if I'm upset, gridlocked in an impasse, or simply not seeing eye-to-eye with someone, it can be healthy to tell them or write down something positive. I had a falling out of sorts with someone a few months ago, but when I was in the presence of someone who serves as a bridge between us recently, the person I fell out with enthusiastically said, "Hi, Marquez" when she heard I was with our bridge on the other side of their phone call. She neutralized my stubbornness with an olive branch. I know that took courage. It rearranged my empathy.

Mindful Appreciation: Practice being present and appreciating the beauty in everyday moments. How arduous do the distractions we're submerged in make it for us to be still? My connecting flight between Phoenix, Arizona and Portland, Oregon was cancelled during a trip a few years ago. Sitting in the shuttle, fuming, the driver, who was an elder asked me where I was headed. He listened to me carp at having to be delayed for a day. I was eager to get to Portland to see a close friend and some family, but the delay made me presume some mindful appreciation. The elder let me finish before turning around with a smile on his face saying, "Young man, never worry about having to sit down. Who knows, that could be an inexplicable thing that rerouted what really needed to happen for you, and not to you." I'll never forget those words. Fixed indelibly in my mental rolodex, I often recite when things don't go as planned. Things happen for you, not to you.

Focus on Positives: Shift your perspective to focus on what's going well, even in challenging situations. I think one of the most helpful benefits of being an athlete growing up for me was (and is) focusing on what's going well, even in challenging situations. It may sound far-fetched, but I never have played a game of anything where I thought I was going to lose, even against immeasurable odds of deficit. I learned and then trained harder to not succumb to doubt of an outcome until the that buzzer sounded or the final score was tallied. An older athlete I looked up to named Val Hill once told me when I was fourteen that basketball was a metaphor of life— you get out of it what you put in it. That has always helped shift my perspective to focus on what's going well, even in challenging situations— the secret is if you give your all, you never lose, you learn.

Acts of Kindness: Perform acts of kindness to cultivate gratitude and contribute to the well-being of others. The best way I can illustrate it is through an experience I had a couple of months ago. I was at the grocery store at the beginning of a long line checking out with the cashier. I had several items that were being scanned as anxious onlookers waited behind me. When the total price flashed across the screen, I dug into my pocket to pull out my wallet. It wasn't there. I realized I had left it on my kitchen table before I left my house and panic mixed when embarrassment started to ensue. As I frantically attempted to save face by searching aimlessly through all my pockets to create a diversion, a serenade of sighs and teeth sucking began to amplify with my humiliation. A sweet voice parted the burgeoning kerfuffle and spoke to me. "Sir don't worry. I'll cover it for you." I turned around and looked. It was a woman with three kids. I immediately refused her offering, but she persisted.

"It's paid, sir." I thanked her and swore I'd see her again one day to reciprocate the gesture. I have yet to see that person, but I damn sure have offered the same every time someone within my presence has been short on a purchase. We're all wealthy when we find a way to perpetuate the well-being of others through acts of kindness.

Gratitude Rituals: Establish routines, like expressing thanks before meals, to embed gratitude into daily life. This one is simple. My most meaningful routine happens every day in the morning when I wake up before every meal, and before I go to sleep. The first words I speak are, "Thank you" when I wake up. Before every meal, I say "Thank you"— for the nourishment of my body and for the removal of all impurities that do not serve me. The last words

I speak every day are "Thank you" for another day to participate in a human experience as a spiritual being.

Gratitude.

The Role of Empathy in Love: How practicing empathy can deepen connections and strengthen romantic relationships.

Once upon a time, a writer went into a studio and saw the walking embodiment of love on two feet. The conversation was psychedelic and infinite possibilities were interwoven within the fabric of their chemistry. They collaborated on some art and went on their separate ways, but serendipity kept conspiring with synchronicities for them to frequent the same paths. Soon, her freckled manuka honey skin tone became his home. Late night walks downtown hallmarked Chicken Shawarma with a side of rice and garlic butter sauce after puff, puff, pass sessions made their rendezvous complete. She kept letting him in and he kept showing up.

If I ever write a romance novel, previous paragraph will be the opening. Ironically, this material was easy to conjure as it was siphoned directly from the inception of the relationship with my partner Fiona. I refer to her as my "partner" because my intentions since we met in her studio are to build together. I learned and firmly believe that "any time two people focus on one thing, it manifests twice as fast. This, like all things in life, works much more effectively of both people sincerely believe in themselves."

When the world collapsed in 2020, other than not being able to hoop because most gyms closed, quarantine was a lay-up line for me as an introvert. I'm also very disciplined in my regiment so I saw 2020 as an opportunity to stop sleeping on my dreams of being a successful, entrepreneurial author. Plan your work and work your plan. Find something you're willing to die for and then live for it. I quietly shut myself inside the house and got busy. I already had scrolls of writings, but the volume exponentially expanded as I attached more fervently to my self-imposed solitary confinement like a barnacle. I feverishly researched EVERYTHING I'd need to know by reading books, watching podcasts and YouTube channels that provided vital information. I have a binder of notes in every color on any entrepreneurial topic imaginable because my intention was INDEPENDENCE. Eleven months of solitude. Social media hiatus (I was only on Facebook at the time). No posts. I didn't have Instagram nor any other social media platform for a page. I started crisscrossing the map on roundtrips to national parks by myself January 2021. By the summer, I bought a brand-new car, ditching the Honda-CRV stagecoach I had run to the ground amassing a small fortune through Uber Eats as a side hustle. At the end of the summer, I emerged as an author, publishing my first book to the astonishment of many because I kept that gift tucked in my back pocket my entire life.

After a couple of bestselling books, my dreams started actualizing rapidly. I met Fiona in 2022. In 2023 when we started seeing each other, I told her these words verbatim, "I'm not leaving my purpose for nobody, and if I can't build with you, and you can't build with me, we're wasting each other's time." As we embarked upon our relationship, the mantra of our meditation at the end of every night became "I choose you" while we sat on the floor facing each other. Choosing each other became our foundation and has become the guidance throughout our continuum of love—a love that is a practice of empathy to strengthen our deep connection. There are seven ways in which Fiona, and I practice empathy with each other.

Active Listening: Take the time to truly listen to your partner's thoughts and feelings without interrupting. I think Fiona and I are both exceptional at holding space for others in a way that heightens our ability to listen—especially to one another. On the palate of interpretation, I tend to devour what others are saying sometimes out of an impatience that ails me like hunger pangs. On the other hand, Fiona will swish around, hold, and tediously taste what others have to offer before slowly digesting it as if she is a sensory evaluator. In other words, I'm more apt to interrupt someone if I discern that they are rendering me to rigamarole. I don't feel bad for this as it grants me freedom from the jaws of garrulity. Fiona is more graceful in enduring vampiric interactions, but I know it drains her as well. Where we learn from each other is that I apply additional patience during conversations by watching her, and she reinforces her boundaries through discourse by observing me. With each other, I imagine an audience would describe our active listening as a discussion between Muhammad Ali and Bob Marley—interestingly enough, one of my favorite icons in Muhammad Ali and one of hers being Bob Marley. My penchant to interrupt is fueled not by insolence, but passion—while she is adroit at alchemizing the rhythm of talk into song that we both find roles to amplify in tune. We get off beat periodically, but we always find our way back to harmony through the instrument of understanding.

Express Understanding: Acknowledge your partner's emotions and let them know you understand how they're feeling. I can't count how many times I've said to Fiona, "I feel you, love." It's my essential way of demonstrating acknowledgement to her immediately. If we are in each other's presence, I wrap my arms around her and recite those words so that the feeling is felt more. I usually follow up by expressing my comprehension of what is transpiring through her vantage point in a way that she feels heard and seen. Fiona does the same, most of the time accompanied by an endearing look that lets me know that she is readily available to acquiesce for emotional support.

Validate Emotions: Confirm that it's okay for your partner to feel the way they do, without judgment. One of the best ways both of us validate emotions in one another is by meeting each other where we are at. If one of us feels dispirited, the other shifts in sync to mirror their emotional positionality. If it's of a low vibration, I insist that one of us going to the other's place of despondency must be a visitation, and not a residence of permanency. When one is down, the other must lift their partner. It's much easier when the one being lifted doesn't feel judged. If Fiona or I feel judged initially, we communicate then remedy the misunderstanding by reinforcing the practice of our partnership.

Offer Support: Be there for your partner in both good and challenging times, offering assistance and encouragement. I read somewhere that couples that work out together tend to excel in areas of problem solving, critical thinking, and situational awareness. Fiona and I have worked out in the park together, lifted weights, and go on strenuous hikes. Working out together serves as a microcosm of life's challenging times because offering assistance and encouragement are essential during workout sessions with a partner. When we fall into a rut of difficulty, we often opt for a hike on one of our most frequented mountains. The incline of the mountain gives us the opportunity to cathartically climb and leave what no longer serves us at the summit. Walking down from the summit is usually a process of exhalation that liberates us from the disagreement and frustration we were saddled with before we embarked upon our scale of the hill. The anatomy of our bond has crucially aided by these types of exercises.

Empathetic Body Language: Non-verbal cues like eye contact, nodding, and comforting gestures convey empathy. As I stated earlier, one of the more powerful acts of empathy Fiona and I use is from sitting on the floor at night while facing each other. This is pivotal for our empathetic body language. It's tough to do this to begin with but imagine doing it with your partner while you are upset with each other. Amazingly, it deescalates. Eye contact at close range accesses another dimension of healing and reflects a truth of humility that seeks peace, with love. In addition, empathetic body language facilitates the intimacy necessitated for ongoing togetherness. I've never experienced this type of elevated communication in a relationship—a key factory that ascertains the fate of many relationships.

Share Vulnerabilities: Open-up about your own feelings and experiences to create a deeper connection. What creates a deeper connection for me, and Fiona is indubitably the vulnerability that binds our union. We've never had the privilege of delaying transparency—naked of anything clandestine as if the forbidden apple of Eden was handled by both of us simultaneously the moment, we shook hands for the first time. In the past, it seemed as if I met the other person for the first time at the end of the relationship, hidden truths shrouded in secrecy that patterned my behaviors in response to an anticipatory familiar outcome. It's comforted me to know that I can share those very thoughts to Fiona in a safe space, and she knows that she can echo fears from her auditorium of truth equally the same.

Apologize and Forgive: When conflicts arise, apologize sincerely, and forgive your partner to foster a compassionate environment. Being able to apologize and forgive can single-handedly make or break a relationship. From my experience, when it is genuine, an apology and forgiveness has proven to be the panacea of any stalemate. The feeling must be mutual and with Fiona, I'm fortunate in that we both are attuned to the feelings and emotions of those around us—chiefly each other as empaths.

www.ingramcontent.com/pod-product-compliance
Lightning Source LLC
Chambersburg PA
CBHW050549160726
48003CB00002B/817